Lewis Hine

Photographer of
Americans at Work

Declaration of Independence
By the Children of America in Mines and Factories and Workshops Assembled

Lewis Wickes Hine's documentary photography helped promote the cause of the National Child Labor Committee, which published this declaration in 1913:

WHEREAS, We, Children of America, are declared to have been born free and equal, and

WHEREAS, We are yet in bondage in this land of the free; are forced to toil the long day or the long night, with no control over the conditions of labor, as to health or safety or hours or wages, and with no right to the rewards of our service, therefore be it

RESOLVED, I — That childhood is endowed with certain inherent and inalienable rights, among which are freedom from toil for daily bread; the right to play and to dream; the right to the normal sleep of the night season; the right to an education, that we may have equality of opportunity for developing all that there is in us of mind and heart.

RESOLVED, II — That we declare ourselves to be helpless and dependent; that we are and of right ought to be dependent, and that we hereby present the appeal of our helplessness that we may be protected in the enjoyment of the rights of childhood.

RESOLVED, III — That we demand the restoration of our rights by the abolition of child labor in America.

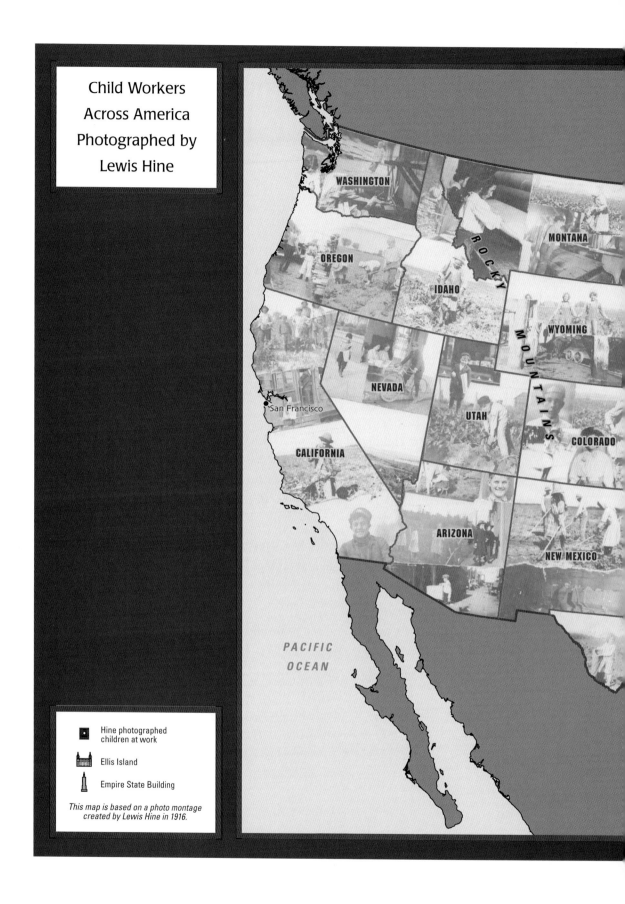

Child Workers
Across America
Photographed by
Lewis Hine

WASHINGTON

OREGON

IDAHO

ROCKY

MONTANA

WYOMING

M O U N T A I N S

NEVADA

•San Francisco

UTAH

COLORADO

CALIFORNIA

ARIZONA

NEW MEXICO

PACIFIC
OCEAN

Hine photographed
children at work

Ellis Island

Empire State Building

*This map is based on a photo montage
created by Lewis Hine in 1916.*

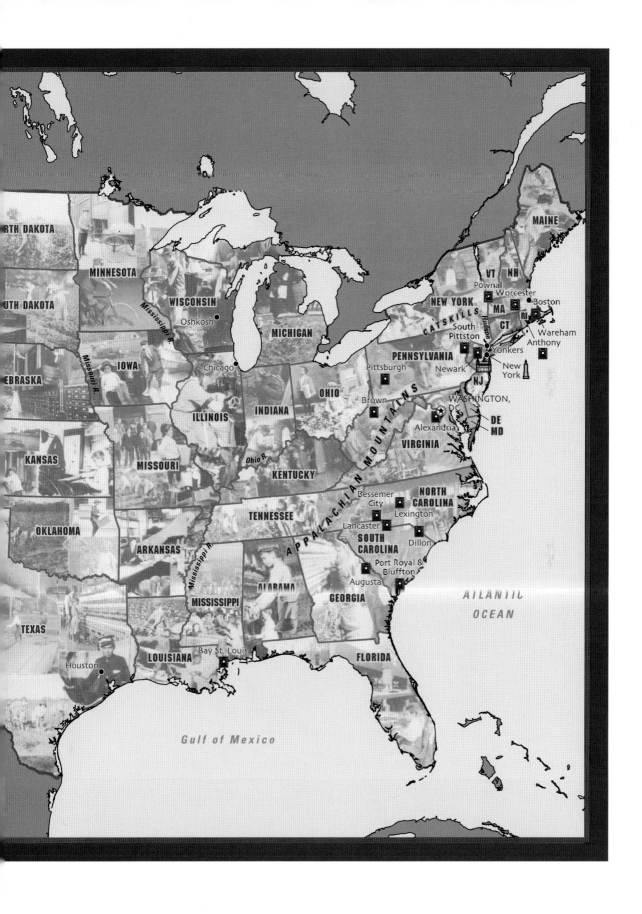

NORTH DAKOTA

MINNESOTA

SOUTH DAKOTA

WISCONSIN

Oshkosh

MICHIGAN

MAINE

VT NH
Pownal
Worcester
Boston
NEW YORK
MA
RI
CATSKILLS
South
Pittston
Wareham
Anthony
Hudson
Yonkers
New York

NEBRASKA

IOWA

Mississippi R.

Missouri R.

Chicago

PENNSYLVANIA
Pittsburgh
Newark
NJ

CT

ILLINOIS

INDIANA

OHIO

Brown

WASHINGTON,
DC
Alexandria

DE
MD

KANSAS

MISSOURI

Ohio R.

KENTUCKY

VIRGINIA

APPALACHIAN MOUNTAINS

NORTH
CAROLINA
Bessemer
City
Lexington
Lancaster
Dillon

OKLAHOMA

ARKANSAS

TENNESSEE

SOUTH
CAROLINA
Port Royal &
Bluffton
Augusta

Mississippi R.

TEXAS

MISSISSIPPI

ALABAMA

GEORGIA

ATLANTIC
OCEAN

Houston

LOUISIANA
Bay St. Louis

FLORIDA

Gulf of Mexico

Map 9

Lewis Hine was eleven years old when this portrait was made.

CHAPTER ONE

The Great Social Peril

The great social peril is darkness and ignorance.
—Lewis Hine

In 1910, a shy, slim photographer stood in front of a large audience which sat in hushed silence. They were stunned by the images that he had just shown them. The photographer had used a magic lantern—the forerunner of the slide projector—to project photographs that had been reproduced on glass plates onto a screen. Shocking images of children—America's children—engaged in backbreaking labor filled the darkened room. Over 2 million children under the age of sixteen worked twelve to fourteen hours a day in similar conditions.

One of these children was a little girl named Sadie, who stood in front of a giant spinning machine, working in a mill where the heat and the dust made breathing very difficult. Others were boys who worked deep inside the Pennsylvania coal mines as trappers, opening the doors from the mines to let out the cars filled with coal. Day after day, they breathed in black coal dust, which coated their lungs and their faces with soot.

Some younger children were breaker boys, sitting outside the mines over coal chutes and taking out pieces of stone that could not be sold because they would not burn. Their fingers were constantly cut by the coal flowing down the shoot. "While I was there," the photographer said, "two breaker boys fell or were carried into the coal chute, where they were smothered to death."

Some children worked in the tenement buildings of large cities, such as New York and Chicago. There, entire families worked together in poorly lit apartments with no fresh air, making artificial flowers or sewing lace. They earned about $1 a day, six days a week, often working until late in the evening. The lace or the flowers they made were sold to affluent people, such as the ones who sat in the audience listening to the photographer's lecture and looking at his pictures. They seemed to have little or no idea of the working conditions that they saw on the screen.

"The great social peril is darkness and ignorance," the photographer wrote. His goal was to educate his audience and increase their understanding of children's working conditions. Mostly, he let the subjects speak for themselves as they looked directly into his camera and communicated their stories. But these were not sad victims. They were proud children whose voices were heard through the pictures and descriptions provided by the soft-spoken photographer.

The United States was in the midst of an industrial revolution, which had begun during the nineteenth century. Factories had sprung up across the country. Deep mines had been dug to provide large supplies of coal that could fuel the new manufacturing plants, and cities had grown to house the hundreds of thousands of workers needed for

"Making lace collars at home, New York, New York." Lewis Wickes Hine, 1911

Immigrant families made lace in their dreary tenement apartments for $1 a day.

"Some adolescents in a Georgia Cotton Mill, Georgia." Lewis Wickes Hine, 1909

Hine photographed young mill workers who used their meager pay to help support their families.

America's industries. While some entrepreneurs became rich during industrialization, many other people worked for low wages and long hours in the mines, the factories, or in their own homes. Adults and children worked side by side to earn enough to feed their families. There were no laws protecting the health and safety of workers and no laws preventing child labor.

As his audience soon realized, the young photographer who stood before them possessed a genius for capturing these working people with his camera. But his photographs also were designed to persuade his viewers that any society that allowed young children to work under such terrible conditions must be changed. Through this powerful presentation and other pictures that he had produced, the photographer created the first American photo stories—a visual documentary aimed at bringing social reform and changing the lives of child workers. He called it "social photography."

The photographer's name was Lewis Wickes Hine.

Child workers put in long days in the dusty coal mines.

Two-year-old Lewis Hine stands next to the drum his father
carried as a young drummer boy during the American Civil War.

CHAPTER TWO

Becoming a Photographer

> The highest aim of the artist is to have something
> to relate and to know how to select the right
> things to reproduce that story.
> —*Lewis Hine*

Lewis Wickes Hine grew up in Oshkosh, Wisconsin. Settled in the mid-1800s, Oshkosh had become a prosperous center of the lumber and furniture industries. In the center of town, Douglas Hull Hine and his wife, Sarah, ran a busy restaurant. Before coming to Oshkosh, Sarah had been a schoolteacher, and Douglas had served as a drummer in the Union Army during the American Civil War. They had three children, two daughters and a son. Lewis, the youngest, was born in 1874.

As he grew up, Lewis watched his parents work long hours to make their business a success. Then, his stable family life suddenly came to an end in 1892, when his father was accidentally killed. Lewis finished high school and immediately went to work at a local furniture factory, earning $4 for a six-day, eighty-hour workweek. It was not much money, but Lewis's income helped support his mother.

When a depression hit America in 1893 and the furniture company went bankrupt, Lewis Hine was forced to look for other work. He drifted through a series of jobs, working as a delivery boy, a salesman, and a janitor at a bank, where he was eventually promoted to the position of secretary to the bank's head cashier. "I was neither physically nor temperamentally fitted for any of these jobs," Hine wrote later.

Along the way, Hine met Professor Frank Manny, who taught at the Oshkosh State Normal School, a teachers' college. Manny became his mentor and persuaded Hine to take classes at the teachers' college. Hine also studied drawing and sculpture and attended the University of Chicago, where he took education courses.

In 1901, Manny left Oshkosh to become superintendent of the Ethical Culture

Hine grew up in the town of Oshkosh, Wisconsin, shown here in about 1850, in a painting by Louis Kurz.

School in New York City. The school's curriculum combined high school academic courses with vocational training. Many of the students were the children of immigrants, millions of whom were coming to the United States from Europe. The largest number of immigrants came to New York City, where they found homes and jobs in the city's densely packed neighborhoods. Most of these immigrants came from Central Europe, and they spoke little or no English. At the Ethical Culture School, immigrant children learned English, mathematics, and the other skills necessary for them to find work after graduation.

Manny invited several teachers from the Oshkosh State Normal School to accompany him to New York. He also invited Lewis Hine. Hine became a teacher of geography and nature studies, and almost immediately he demonstrated his skills as a gifted teacher. Hine was a wonderful actor and entertained his students while he taught them. In 1904, he briefly returned to Oshkosh, where he married Sara Rich, a woman whom he had met at the Normal School.

Meanwhile, Hine was attending New York University, where he earned a master's degree in education in 1905. During his early years at the Ethical Culture School, Hine also began experimenting with a camera. Frank Manny was looking for someone to record school events, and Hine's expertise—although it was, at first, very limited—fit perfectly into Manny's plans.

"I had long wanted to use the camera for records and you were the only one who seemed to see what I was after," Manny later wrote to Hine. "You were adequate, ready to learn and used not only me but everyone in sight who was willing to help." Hine read how-to magazines, which contained instructions on photography. He also learned how to develop photographs using chemicals in a darkroom. At this time, photography was little more than a half century old in the United States. Pioneering work in the field had been done by men such as Mathew Brady. Brady had created photographic portraits of political leaders such as President Abraham Lincoln, as well as vivid battle scenes of the American Civil War.

Hine began photographing school events, which included dances and club meetings, as well as students working in the school carpentry shop and taking instruction in an art class. He also started teaching his students how to operate a camera. The program was partly designed as vocational training. It taught students how to become photographers, providing them with a possible occupation after they graduated from school. But even more important, Hine believed that by using a camera, his students would learn how to see the world around them and interpret it for others. They photographed the ships in New York Harbor, proud symbols of American commerce, as well as the natural world of trees and flowers, which Hine loved very much. Most of the students had never been outside New York City before, so the world of nature offered a new experience for them.

HINE ON PHOTOGRAPHY

About his early experiences as a photographer, Hine wrote, "A good photograph is not a mere reproduction of an object or group of objects—it is an interpretation of Nature, a reproduction of impressions made upon the photographer which he desires to repeat to others." He added, "The highest aim of the artist is to have something to relate and to know how to select the right things to reproduce that story." As these words indicate, Hine saw himself as a teacher, using his photographs to tell a story and make an impact on his viewers.

Hine reads in his apartment in 1900. He learned about the art of photography from books and magazines.

The children of immigrants attended the Ethical Culture School, where Hine taught photography.

Hine loved the outdoors and took his students into the countryside to enjoy it.

Finally, Hine wanted his students to sharpen their perceptions and discipline themselves to look at the world more closely—skills that would help them later in life. "This sharpening of vision," he wrote, "to a better appreciation of the beauties [of nature] I consider the best fruit of the whole work." The students took photographs, developed them in a darkroom, and then studied the portraits of the natural world that they had captured in their pictures. Eventually, Hine published articles about his unique camera course, so that others could learn about it. "The fundamental aim of the course is to help the pupils to a better appreciation of good photography and how to attain it."

He also wrote about his love of nature. In an article for the *Oshkosh Northwestern* in 1903, Hine described a trip he had taken to the Catskill Mountains of upstate New York. "I spent the night above the clouds and awoke in the morning to an experience new to me. It was a clear, sunny day, with bright, blue sky overhead. Below . . . was a mass of white cumulus clouds stretching away to the horizon and looking like a great tempestuous sea."

From the early photographs, taken while at the Ethical Culture School, Hine and Manny began to look to the wider world. This opened up a new vista for the young photographer and transformed him into a photojournalist—someone who tells an important story through pictures.

Ellis Island in New York Harbor was the main entry
point for European immigrants.

CHAPTER THREE

Hine at Ellis Island

Our air was full of the new social spirit.
–Frank Manny

In 1904, Lewis Hine began to use his camera for new projects, which he later described as "changing the educational efforts from the schoolroom to the world." He first turned his attention to Ellis Island, which was near his classroom at the Ethical Culture School. Lying in New York Harbor about a half mile from the Statue of Liberty, Ellis Island was opened as an immigrant station in 1892. It became the main entry point for immigrants coming by ship to the United States from Europe. Hine decided to photograph some of these immigrants as they arrived in America.

For millions of immigrants—many of them from Eastern and Southern Europe — America offered the promise of hope. They had left behind poverty, persecution for religious beliefs, and little or no chance of obtaining an education or a better job. They had come to America hoping to find all the opportunities that had been denied them at home.

As his ship entered New York Harbor, Greek immigrant Doukanie Papandreos recalled, "I saw the Statue of Liberty, and I said to myself, 'Lady, you're beautiful. You opened your arms and you get all the foreigners here. Give me a chance to prove that I am worth it, to do something to become somebody in America.'"

Once they arrived at Ellis Island, the immigrants went to the main building—the central examination center of the U.S. Bureau of Immigration. The noise was deafening, as thousands of people crowded together, speaking a variety of languages. Doctors checked men, women, and children to ensure that they were not crippled or carrying an infectious disease. Anyone who was sick went to the island's hospital or had to return to Europe. The immigrants were asked questions in their native language, including their name and the type of work they did. They also were tested for their ability to read and do simple arithmetic. The inspectors wanted to make sure that the immigrants could support themselves once they entered the United States.

Beginning the Project

Hine's wife, Sara, recalled that the idea of photographing immigrants began for him with an "urge to capture and record some of the most picturesque of what many of our friends were talking about." While doing his graduate work at Columbia University, Hine had met Arthur and Paul Kellogg, who were editors at a magazine called *Charities and the Commons*.

The Kelloggs were among the many reformers during the period who called themselves Progressives. They were concerned about improving the living conditions of new immigrants and other Americans, many of whom lived in squalid slums in New York and other large cities.

Poverty had always been present in the United States, but until this time most Americans believed that the poor had only their own laziness to blame for their living conditions. As industrialization spread during the late nineteenth century and cities grew larger, the number of poor increased. Reformers, such as the Kelloggs and other Progressives, recognized that most of the poor were employed. But they were paid extremely low wages by employers who were growing rich off their labor. Because of their low incomes, many families were forced to live in tenement buildings owned by slumlords who exploited them.

The Progressives began gathering statistics about the number of people who lived in poverty, their low wages, their lack of education, and the conditions in their run-down tenement housing. Many of the Progressives were professional social workers who recorded information about the poor families whom they served in America's cities. By bringing this information to the attention of political leaders, the Progressives hoped to make changes in American society.

Lewis Hine caught the spirit of American reform. As Frank Manny put it, "Our air was full of the new social spirit." Manny and Hine also wanted to use the photographs of Ellis Island as teaching tools for the students who attended the Ethical Culture School. Many of them were the children of newly arrived immigrants, and Manny wanted them to be proud of their heritage. After all, they had come to the United States just as the Pilgrims had three centuries before. Years later, Manny wrote

"Climbing into America, immigrants at Ellis Island." Lewis Wickes Hine, 1905

In 1904, Lewis Hine began photographing immigrants at Ellis Island.

to Hine, "Do you recall our talking about a Pilgrim Celebration and a little Russian [student] said he was thankful that the Pilgrims [had] landed on Plymouth Rock. I said I wanted the children of later days to feel equal regard for . . . Ellis Island."

The Art of Photography

In 1904, Hine and Manny made their first trip to Ellis Island. Picture taking at the beginning of the twentieth century was far more complicated than simply snapping a picture with a small camera and a built-in flash. Hine and Manny carried 50 pounds of equipment, including a large box-shaped camera and a wooden tripod. Hine also lugged a collection of heavy glass plates in a leather case, which he carried over his shoulder. He inserted a plate into the camera each time he wanted to make a picture.

Since the main rooms at Ellis Island were dark, Hine needed a flash to provide more light. This was provided by flash powder, made of a combination of magnesium and a chemical called potassium chlorate, which was spread over a metal pan. The pan was held in the air, and the powder was ignited by a flint wheel or an electrical wire that provided a spark. The powder exploded with a bang—the origin of the term "shooting a picture"—and, at the same time, the photographer took the picture by opening the shutter on the camera.

Setting up a shot took time. Since most of the immigrants did not speak English, Hine had to use sign language to indicate that he wanted to take their picture. Most were "bewildered," as he put it. After all, they had just arrived in New York after a long voyage across rough seas to a strange new land. First, Hine had to persuade a group of immigrants to stop so that he could take their picture. Then he had to set up the camera and put in the glass plate as Manny prepared the flash.

"By that time most of the group," Hine recalled, "were either silly or stony or weeping with hysteria because the bystanders had been busy pelting them with advice and comments, and the climax came when you raised the flash pan aloft over them and they waited, rigidly, for the blast. It took all the resources of a hypnotist, a super salesman and a ball pitcher to prepare them to play the game and then to outguess them so most were not either wincing or shutting eyes when the time came to shoot. Naturally, everyone shut his eyes when the flash went off but the fact that their reactions were a little slower than . . . the flash saved the day, usually."

Hine's Photographs

What Hine caught with his camera was the courage of human beings who had taken the risk to come to a new country and begin their lives anew. He also captured the

Despite the challenges of taking a picure in the early days of photography, Hine managed to capture the pathos of the immigrant experience in a single gaze.

anxiety they experienced at encountering America's strangeness, their exhaustion after so long a voyage, and their desire to create a better life, not only for themselves but also for the children who often accompanied them. Hine recorded all of these things by communicating across the language barrier to photograph the unique experiences of individual human beings. As Hine put it, "I have always been more interested in persons than in people."

As one critic of his work put it, "He went to Ellis Island as a school photographer; he left it a master. . . . His pictures are quick with the moment; they show figures in

"Family of Mrs. Mette making flowers in a very dirty tenement, New York." Lewis Wickes Hine, 1911

Hine's photograph of the Mettes showed that children of all ages had to work to support their families. Thirteen-year-old Josephine Mette told Hine that she had worked in an embroidery factory the previous summer.

the act of experiencing Ellis Island.... Put another way, he allowed his subjects room for *their* self-expression. This is something that cannot be taught, cannot be reduced to rules." Hine was so excited by his work at Ellis Island that he returned again and again over the next few years, taking a total of about 200 pictures. In 1907 alone, over one million immigrants came through Ellis Island, and Hine preserved many of them in his photographs. Today, these people speak to us from another era, expressing emotions that form part of the universal human experience.

Exposing Life in the Slums

Hine did not forget about the immigrants after they left Ellis Island. He followed them into the tenements of the Lower East Side of New York City.

He was not the first person to do this. During the 1880s, journalist Jacob Riis had set out to expose the poverty experienced by many of the people who lived in New York. At first, he told their stories in newspaper articles, but, as he later said, "I wrote, but it seemed to make no impression." Then, Riis learned to take pictures. He brought his camera and a flash inside the dark tenement buildings, where people lived and worked.

Finally, in 1890, Riis published his book *How the Other Half Lives.* No one had ever before captured the poor in photographs. As author Vicki Goldberg wrote, "Rather than prettying up or sentimentalizing poverty, Riis recorded every bit of clutter, rubbish and grit, every peeling wall, overcrowded bed and tattered garment. . . . He photographed entire families, parents and children, working together in tight quarters as if their lives depended on it—which they did. . . . The world he depicted was in danger of coming apart, if it did not suffocate first in dirt and misery."

Riis was among the first to use photographs as a form of social documentary—that is, to record the living and working conditions of a large group of Americans. He not only published his photographs but also lectured to large audiences, turning his pictures into slides and projecting them with a magic lantern.

Hine followed in the footsteps of Jacob Riis. In his photographs, Hine portrayed immigrants such as, in his words, "Mrs. Palontona and 13-year-old daughter, working on pillow lace in dirty kitchen of their tenement home. They were both very illiterate. Mother is making fancy lace and girl sold me lace she worked on."

In another photograph, Hine captured the "Family of Mrs. Mette making flowers in a dirty tenement. Josephine, 13 years, helps outside of school hours until 9 P.M. sometimes. She is soon to be 14 and expects to go to work in an embroidery factory, then. Says she worked in that factory all last summer."

Not only in tenements but also in factories across America, many of the workers were children like Josephine Mette. These children became the next subjects of Hine's pioneering work as a social photographer. Through his pictures, he would create a timeless documentary that speaks as powerfully to us today as it did to Americans over a century ago.

In his most brilliant and haunting photographic essays,
Hine publicized the plight of America's child workers.

CHAPTER FOUR

The Tragedy of Child Labor

While photographs may not lie, liars may photograph.
—Lewis Hine

President Theodore Roosevelt called them "muckrakers." They were journalists who wrote stories about the greed and dishonesty that lay at the heart of American business and government. Ida Tarbell wrote a series of articles for *McClure's* magazine exposing the deals that John D. Rockefeller made as the head of Standard Oil to gain a monopoly in the oil business. Lincoln Steffens wrote about St. Louis, where shrewd entrepreneurs received government contracts by bribing city officials. And Upton Sinclair published a book in 1906 called *The Jungle*, which exposed the unsafe working conditions and the lack of quality inspections in the meatpacking industry. The writings of the muckrakers brought reforms—including new laws aimed at stopping monopolies and the Meat Inspection Act.

Among the journalists at the center of the reform movement were Lewis Hine's friends Arthur and Paul Kellogg, who were editors at *Charities and the Commons*. In 1906, Hine wrote to Frank Manny, "I have just hunted up Mr. Kellogg, Editor of *Charities*, and have started him thinking about the advisability of hiring a man . . . to do photography for the magazine."

In the early twentieth century, the use of photographs was a new phenomenon in American magazines. Most periodicals used illustrations, drawn by artists, to accompany a story. These were considered more artistic, while photographs seemed crude and not appropriate for fine magazines and journals. Nevertheless, *Charities and the Commons* began running photographs, including some of the pictures taken by Lewis

MEATPACKING

By the beginning of the twentieth century, Chicago meatpackers were producing more than 80 percent of all the meat eaten in the United States. Large meatpackers, such as Armour and Swift, had over 25,000 people employed in their companies—many of them newly arrived European immigrants. Not only did the companies process meat for American consumers, meat by-products were used to create soap, fertilizer, oleomargarine, and glue. But conditions in the meatpacking industry were unsanitary, with dead rats sometimes being packed into sausage.

After Upton Sinclair exposed these conditions in his book *The Jungle*, President Theodore Roosevelt vowed to make immediate changes to protect the health of the American people. In response, Congress established the Food and Drug Administration and passed the Meat Inspection Act of 1906. This enabled the government to demand many more meat inspections and prevent any product from being sold if it did not meet thorough health requirements.

Hine at Ellis Island. Hine was pioneering a new approach to journalism called the photo story. This was a series of photographs with captions that told a story.

The Plight of Child Workers

Around 1906, Arthur Kellogg suggested to Hine that he might do freelance photography and create photo stories for the National Child Labor Committee (NCLC). Founded in 1905, the NCLC was dedicated to eliminating child labor in the United States. Although some states had passed legislation outlawing child labor, these laws were not enforced. As a result, approximately 2 million children worked in mines, factories, and agricultural fields. Children were paid less than adult workers, which had the effect of reducing wages for everyone. In addition, they often were injured on the job—falling in large cotton looms where they lost toes and fingers or even their lives.

The plight of America's working children was a primary concern of the reform movement. Reformers were convinced that children would have no chance to raise themselves out of poverty unless they could stay in school and receive an education. This was impossible if they were forced to go to work to support their families. But most people were not aware that so many children were actually employed in American industry, nor did they realize the danger involved in their work.

"A view of the Pennsylvania Breaker. South Pittston." Lewis Wickes Hine. 1911

"Harold Walker, 5 years old, picks cotton on a farm in Commanche County, Oklahoma." Lewis Wickes Hine. 1916

Breaker boys risked their health and their lives in dangerous mine work.

Hine traveled to the South to create a timeless photo of a child working in a cotton field.

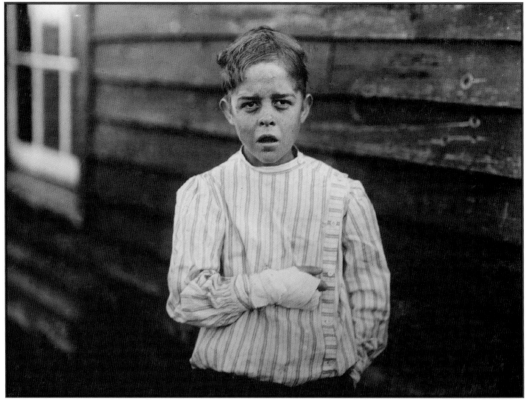

Many children were injured, and some lost
their lives working in factories and mines.

The NCLC was dedicated to publicizing this situation. Its inspectors went into factories, mines, and fish canneries to expose the conditions of child workers. Then the NCLC printed the inspectors' reports in its brochures and pamphlets to expose the tragedy of child labor. But, as the NCLC soon discovered, words alone lacked impact.

Hine and the NCLC

In 1906, Hine went to work for the NCLC as its first freelance photographer. While conducting investigations for the committee, he also took photographs of what he saw. Their impact was much greater than words—providing evidence for readers to see the lives of children who were forced to work in dirty, dangerous conditions. But Hine realized that he had to be careful with his photographs, "to be double sure that [my] photo-data was 100% pure—no retouching or fakery of any kind." He did not want anyone to accuse him of creating false evidence.

Hine's first photo story for the NCLC, produced in 1907, was titled "Night Scenes in the City of Brotherly Love," an exposé of child workers in Philadelphia. In a brochure

Young newsboys were proud of the money they earned delivering newspapers.

made of a series of fold-out panels, Hine presented photos of street vendors, newsboys, and box makers. Each panel was labeled with a different hour of the evening, beginning at 8 P.M. and ending at 4 A.M. Each photograph had a caption. For example, under a picture of a boy delivering newspapers, Hine wrote, "From ten Saturday evening to two Sunday morning he makes about 20 cents." In each of Hine's pictures, the children appear in bright light, surrounded by darkness. The camera and the flash brought light, so that the people who saw the pictures would finally leave the "darkness" of ignorance and understand the conditions in which the children lived and worked. "Light is required," Hine added. "Light! Light in floods."

The Survey and the NCLC

In 1907, Paul Kellogg received a request from the city authorities in Pittsburgh, Pennsylvania, to conduct a survey of working conditions among the poor. Pittsburgh was a leading center of the steel industry. Among the artists and social workers whom Kellogg asked to travel to Pittsburgh was Lewis Hine. The investigators interviewed steel

Children who should have been in school spent
their days working in dusty cotton mills.

workers and compiled statistics, while the artists sketched steelworkers and Hine photographed them. In 1908 and 1909, *Charities and the Commons* devoted three issues to the results of the survey. Afterward, the journal changed its name to *The Survey*. Among the articles was a photo story by Lewis Hine called "Immigrant Types in the Steel District."

In 1908, Hine left the Ethical Culture School to become a professional photographer. It was a risky decision, leaving a full-time job with a guaranteed salary for freelance photography. Hine had no idea how much money he might make. Early in the year, he went to Washington, D.C., where he photographed poor families living in the slums. These pictures appeared in a book titled *Neglected Neighbors: Stories of Life in the Alleys, Tenements, and Shanties of the National Capital*, written by Charles Weller, and published in 1909.

In August, the NCLC gave Hine a salary of $100 per month and paid his expenses to travel to Indiana, Ohio, North Carolina, South Carolina, and West Virginia. Usually, the committee sent a team of three people to investigate working conditions—a writer, a photographer, and a witness to verify their facts. In that way, no one could claim later that the information was not entirely accurate. "[The authorities] try to get around [the photographs] by crying 'Fake,'" said Hine, "but therein lies the value of the date and a witness."

Among Hine's subjects was Sadie Pfeifer, a young girl only 4 feet tall. Hine photographed her in front of a large cotton loom to show the contrast between the child and the machinery. In another photo, Hine captured an eleven-year-old spinner in North Carolina taking a break from her work to look longingly out a window. "A moment's glimpse of the outer world," was the caption that Hine put under his picture. He noted that she had started working when she was ten years old.

In 1909, a collection of his photographs with captions, titled *Day Laborers Before Their Time*, told the stories of the children in the pictures. The NCLC used Hine's photos in their brochures and on posters that graphically portrayed children at work. Early in 1909, Hine attended the NCLC Annual Conference in Chicago, which also featured his work. While visiting Chicago, Hine photographed Hull House, founded in 1889 by Jane Addams.

HULL HOUSE AND JANE ADDAMS

Born in 1860, Jane Addams graduated from Rockford College in 1881 at a time when very few women received a higher education. Eight years later, she established Hull House in Chicago with her close friend Ellen Gates Star. For $60 per month, they rented a large house that had been owned by Charles Hull.

Located in a poor section of Chicago, Hull House provided educational programs for immigrants newly arrived from Europe. Volunteers ran classes in subjects such as history and literature, and they gave cooking and sewing lessons. Some of the immigrants at Hull House put on events that featured food and music from their own countries. Hull House also set up bathing facilities for poor tenement families, a daycare center for the children of working parents, and a gymnasium.

During the early twentieth century, Addams led efforts to bring reforms in child labor conditions, housing for the poor, and education for all.

Hine captured not only child laborers in his photos but also the conditions under which they worked, as in this glass factory.

After leaving Chicago, Hine spent the rest of the year traveling to mills in New England and fish canning plants along the Gulf of Mexico. He also photographed young glass workers in New Jersey. Many manufacturers were not eager to admit Hine and allow him to photograph their operations. Therefore, he had to convince them that he had arrived at their plant for another reason. Hine was a marvelous actor. Sometimes, he would carry a stack of bibles with him and tell a plant foreman that he was a bible salesman. Or Hine would explain that he was an industrial photographer and had come to a mill to photograph the manufacturing machinery. Then, he would pose a young child in front of a large machine and take pictures.

In 1910, the NCLC hired Hine as a full-time photographer, paying him $3,000 per year plus expenses. "I am sure I am right in my choice of work," Hine wrote later. "My child labor photos have already set the authorities to work to see if such things can be possible." His photographs had already begun appearing in newspapers and magazines, where they were seen by countless Americans.

During the next few years, Hine traveled thousands of miles, visiting manufacturing sites and mines and taking pictures. In 1911, he was accompanied by his wife, Sara, who helped write reports and acted as a witness. According to their records, they covered "13 cotton mills, 10 knitting mills, 5 silk mills, 3 woolen mills, and glass and shoe factories." They also traveled to sardine canneries in Maine and cranberry fields in

ADDIE CARD

In 1910, Hine photographed Addie Card, a spinner at a mill in North Pownal, Vermont. This image is considered one of his most famous photographs. Addie Card even appeared on a U.S. postage stamp in 1998, 100 years after she was born.

Addie's mother had died in 1900, her father had disappeared, and the two-year-old had been taken in by her grandmother. At age twelve, Addie was already working in the cotton mill.

Hine photographed Addie standing in front of the spinning machine that she worked on, in bare feet, looking directly at the camera. Although she wore a torn, stained smock, Addie still appeared proud and determined, like so many other children whom Hine photographed.

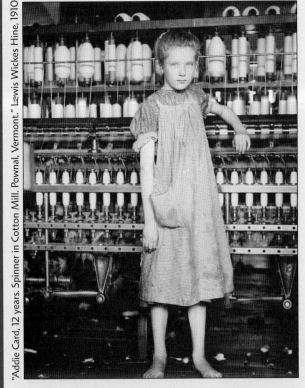

"Addie Card, 12 years. Spinner in Cotton Mill. Pownal, Vermont." Lewis Wickes Hine, 1910

At age fifteen, Addie married another worker at the mill, Edward Hatch. He later left the mill to join the U.S. Navy. The couple had one child, a daughter, born in 1919. Addie died in 1993. She was ninety-four years old. Her daughter died nine years later in 2002.

When Hine visited factories, he told employers that he wanted to photograph their machinery, but his real subjects were the child workers.

Time Exposures by Lewis Wickes Hine, 1908–1912

"Fanny ßreto. Said 9 years old. Was picking with her father on a private bog near ßang's bog. Wareham, Massachusetts."

"7-year old Rosie. Regular oyster shucker. Her second year at it. Illiterate. Works all day. Shucks only a few pots a day. Varn & Platt Canning Co. ßluffton, South Carolina."

"Maud Daly, five years old. Grace Daly, three years old. Each picks about one pot of shrimp a day for the Peerless Oyster Co. The youngest said to be the fastest worker. ßay St. Louis, Mississippi."

"Maple Mills, Dillon, S.C. Soarbar Seris, has worked off and on in the mill for 5 years. Winds. Gets 70 cents and up. 'Recon I'm about 14.' Didn't look it. Has worked more nights than day time. Dillon, South Carolina."

"Young Driver in Mine: Had been driving one year. (7 A.M. to 5:30 P.M. Daily) ßrown Mine, ßrown, West Virginia."

"One of the young spinners in the Quidwick Co. Mill. Anthony, R.I. (A Polish boy Willie) who was taking his noon rest in a doffer-box. Anthony, Rhode Island."

"Joseph and Rosy, 10 and 8 yrs. old. He sells [newspapers] until evening. She is one of 5 or 6 girls who sell (afternoons). Newark, New Jersey."

"Nearly 9 A.M. Girl (about 8 yrs. old) carrying sack of hose supporters home, a long distance and she had to run to get home in time for school. Up hill and tiring work, resting frequently. Worcester, Massachusetts."

"Workers in the Nokomis Cotton Mill. The smallest boy said he was 11 years old and makes 50 cents a day. Been doffing there for some months. The band boy who seems much younger would not be photographed. Lexington, North Carolina."

"A little spinner in Globe Cotton Mill. The overseer admitted she was regularly employed. Augusta, Georgia."

"Eldridge Bernard, 11 yrs. old. Buster Smith, 6 yrs. old. Route boys of Newark. Colored. Taken at 4 P.M. Location: Newark, New Jersey."

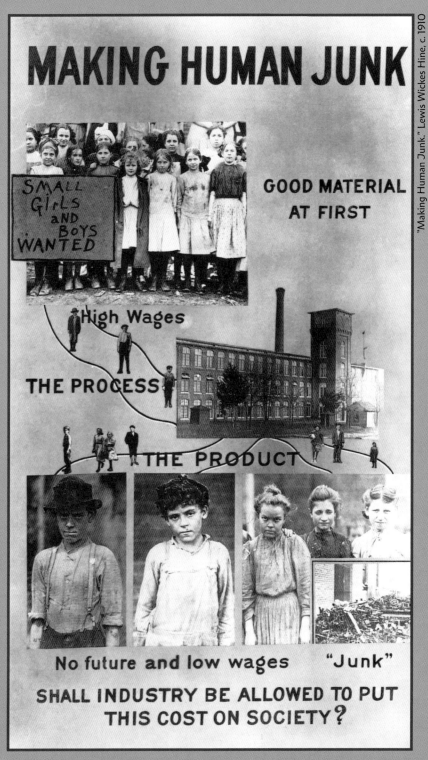

Hine pioneered the photo story, which combined
a series of pictures with captions.

Massachusetts. The next year, Sara stayed in New York, where she gave birth to a son, Corydon.

Hine's Success

By 1913, Lewis Hine was "considered the most . . . successful photographer of social welfare work in the country." He continued to travel to manufacturing plants in many parts of the United States. He was also in charge of exhibits for the NCLC, designing

THE POWER OF A PHOTOGRAPH

There is an old saying that "a picture is worth a thousand words." Lewis Hine's pictures had the impact of many thousands of words on the people who saw them. As one reporter who attended a conference featuring some of Hine's pictures wrote, "There has been no more convincing proof of the absolute necessity of child labor laws . . . than these pictures showing the suffering, the degradation . . . the utter [lack] of anything that is wholesome in the lives of these poor little wage earners. They speak far more eloquently than any [written] work."

"Newsboy asleep on stairs with papers, Jersey City, New Jersey," Lewis Wickes Hine, 1912

The long workday left most children feeling exhausted.

Children in the tenements had to create their own makeshift baseball fields.

TIME EXPOSURES

To describe his method of arranging pictures, Hine came up with a new term—"time exposures." This described a series of pictures, or photo montages, in different shapes and sizes to accompany an article that Hine composed himself. Several of these time exposures appeared in *The Survey* in 1914. They include "Three Bits of Testimony for the Consumers of Shrimp and Oysters," showing children working in a cannery with descriptions by the photographer. Another time exposure was titled "Girl Workers in a Cotton Mill." Hine also created time exposures about other themes, such as children's activities in the city during the summer. These photos portrayed children playing ball, flying kites, and cooling off at an open fire hydrant.

elaborate photographic displays and captions that depicted the extent of child labor. These pictures proved that, although states did have laws that prohibited child labor, employers paid no attention to them. Hine used his slides to present lectures on child labor, and the NCLC loaned his photographs to groups throughout America that were trying to publicize the conditions of children at work.

Although Hine and the NCLC campaigned to end child labor, progress was slow. In 1912, the U.S. Children's Bureau was established to investigate and report "upon all matters pertaining to the welfare of children." But no national law prohibiting child labor was passed until 1938 as part of the Fair Labor Standards Act. As a result, Hine sometimes found himself saddened that all his work had failed to make substantial changes.

In a pamphlet called *Tasks for the Tenements*, Hine wrote, "tenement [work] seems to me one of the most iniquitous phases of child-slavery that we have. It is then that I come nearest to hysterics, and so, if I seem to be smiling over the subject at any time . . . you may rest assured I would rather weep."

Lewis Hine (standing right) prepares to photograph refugees at an American Red Cross canteen in Paris, France, in 1918.

CHAPTER FIVE

Hine and World War I

If I could tell the story in words, I wouldn't
need to lug around a camera.
—*Lewis Hine*

I n August 1914, Europe plunged into World War I. This brutal conflict, which would claim 9 million casualties over the next four years, pitted Great Britain, France, and Russia—the Allies—against Germany and Austria, known as the Central Powers. During the early years of the war, the United States remained neutral. President Woodrow Wilson and a majority of Americans believed that they had no business becoming involved in a European conflict.

Lewis Hine agreed. In one of his photo stories, he showed the wives and babies of American immigrants. Titled "The Girls They Leave Behind," it included a caption by Hine in which he wrote, "It is estimated that the industrial army of America contains one million reservists subject to call in European armies." Hine believed that if these new American citizens left their jobs, went back to Europe, and served in the war, their families would be left without any means of financial support.

As the war continued, however, public opinion in the United States began to change. The German government launched hundreds of submarines that torpedoed any ship believed to be bringing supplies to the Allies. The ships that were attacked included neutral vessels, some of which were flying the flag of the United States. As a result, many Americans lost their lives at sea. Outraged by Germany's violations of U.S. neutrality, the United States finally declared war on the Central Powers in 1917.

By this time, the focus of Hine's photographic work had shifted. At first, he had continued to take photographs for the National Child Labor Committee. But as World War I dragged on, Americans began to lose interest in reform as their atten-

Hine was a master at photographing people. Some of his subjects were Americans enlisting in the armed forces.

tion shifted to the conflict in Europe. Hine began shooting pictures of American soldiers preparing to go to war. About the same time, Paul Kellogg traveled to Europe to cover the activities of the American Red Cross. During the war, the Red Cross was involved in providing food, medical care, and shelter for the vast numbers of refugees driven from their homes by the fighting.

Early in 1918, Hine asked the NCLC to increase his salary. Instead, the committee decided to reduce his monthly pay from $275 to $200. Meanwhile, Hine had been looking for other work. In France, Major Homer Folks, head of the Red Cross Department of Civil Affairs, needed a photographer. He was probably familiar with Hine's work for the NCLC and *The Survey*. In addition, Folks worked closely with Kellogg, who may have recommended Hine.

Hine's Photographs in Europe

In May 1918, the Red Cross hired Hine. He was filled with excitement about making his first trip abroad. Since the Red Cross was considered part of the American armed forces, Hine became a captain in the U.S. Army and wore a military uniform when taking photographs in Europe. Hine's work began as soon as he reached Paris. By that time, World War I was entering its final stages. Since 1914, the German Army had occupied eastern France. But with the arrival of American troops in Europe, the Allies began to push the enemy back into Germany.

Some of Hine's early photographs portrayed Red Cross activities in the areas around Paris. Using the style that he had perfected in his pictures of child workers, Hine also created poignant portraits of the French people. His intention was to portray their strength in the face of four years of brutal warfare, as well as their determination to rebuild as the war came to an end. One of his most moving portraits features an elderly woman in Le Havre, France, with the caption, "Been waiting in this hut for four years for son to return."

Many of Hine's pictures, not surprisingly, were of French children. He showed a grim-faced boy fishing on the banks of the Seine River in Paris, a lovely little girl wearing a white dress in Normandy, and a delivery boy, with a big smile on his face, pulling a cart in Chateauveaux. One of Hine's most moving portraits features an elderly newspaper seller in Bordeaux, sitting by her newsstand with her dog.

On November 11, 1918, the Germans agreed to a peace treaty, and the war was finally over. On that same day, Hine and Folks left Paris for Italy. Their mission was to conduct a special survey of conditions in postwar Europe. The Red Cross wanted to highlight the destruction caused by the war and persuade Americans to donate large sums of money to help rebuild Europe. Hine's pictures and Folks's commentary were to appear in the Red Cross magazines that were being circulated in the United States. Hine contrasted this work with the pictures he had taken for the NCLC. "I thought I

THE RED CROSS

In 1859, a wealthy Swiss entrepreneur named Henry Dunant happened to be in the Italian town of Solferino when a battle was fought there between the French and Austrian armies. Over 40,000 soldiers were left dead or wounded on the battlefield. Dunant helped provide medical treatment for the wounded soldiers. Five years later, he helped establish the International Committee of the Red Cross. This new organization adopted a red cross as its symbol. In the United States, Clara Barton worked as a nurse on Civil War battlefields during the 1860s. In 1881, she set up the American Red Cross. During World War I, the Red Cross provided medical care for soldiers wounded on battlefields in Europe.

Hine captured the endurance of the French people, such
as this newspaper seller, who endured four years of war.

had done my share of negative documentation," he said. "I wanted to do something
positive." He hoped to improve the social conditions in Europe through his photographs.

In Turin, Hine was awakened at 4 A.M. by the sound of church bells. The Special
Survey Mission then traveled to Rome, where Hine was especially fascinated by the
giant Colosseum—the massive open theater built by the ancient Romans. "I wanted
to camp out there for a week," he commented. "I would like to do a series of photos
here." But Hine and Folks had arrived for an entirely different mission.

They soon left central Italy for Greece and Serbia, which had been devastated by
the war. Hine's photographic methods on this trip were different from those he had
used in the United States. They featured more action shots, taken quickly. To make
these photographs, Hine used a faster shutter speed on his camera—that is, the opening within the camera had to open and close more quickly to let in light and capture
the action. These pictures not only appeared in the *Red Cross Magazine*, they also
were featured in *The Survey*. In addition, Folks was writing a book titled *The Human
Costs of the War* and needed Hine's pictures to illustrate his words. (The book was
published in 1920.)

ARMISTICE CELEBRATIONS

"We left Paris the evening of Nov. 11th, the day the official announcement of the signing of the Armistice [peace agreement] was made," Hine wrote. "Paris had held herself in check up to this moment but when there was no longer any doubt, the people broke loose, flooded the streets in . . . processions, marching, surging, singing, shouting. . . . My taxi crawled along, a gendarme [policeman] would jump and direct us a while, some of the marchers, young and old, would mount the running board [of the taxi] and insist upon shaking hands."

When Hine and Folks arrived in Turin, Italy, there were celebrations there, too. Italy had fought alongside the Allies during the war. "They were still celebrating—bands and crowds surging up and down, groups stopping to [shout] 'Vive Americain' [Long live Americans] at us when they spied our caps."

The armistice on November 11, 1918, brought the
French people into the streets to celebrate victory.

"Group of Poor Children." Lewis Wickes Hine, 1918

Hine described this photograph as "a girl of eight or nine [who] cares for a group of smaller children on the street in Taranto, Italy."

Some of Hine's photos portrayed the desperate conditions of the war refugees. But many of his pictures were more upbeat. A photo story titled "The Child's Burden in the Balkans" pictured children doing various types of work in Serbia and Greece. Unlike his pictures of child workers in the United States, some of these children seemed happy. They were learning a trade, such as becoming a stone worker or a coppersmith, filling jobs left open by adults who had gone off to war.

Early in 1919, Hine and Folks returned to Paris and two months later left on the final leg of the Special Survey Mission. The purpose of this trip was to depict the areas in northeastern France and Belgium that had been occupied by the Germans and ripped apart in some of the war's fiercest fighting. This was a quick ten-day trip, and Hine shot some of his pictures from a car as they were traveling along the roadways. As Folks put it, the trip was designed "to see the conditions of housing, food and employment at this very early stage of reconstruction."

One of Hine's pictures showed a new house constructed by the government amid the rubble of bombed-out buildings to serve as a home for refugees. In another pic-

Opposite: "General view facing on Place de la Republique. Armentieres, France." Lewis Wickes Hine, 1919

Opposite: "Homeless Family in Temporary Shelter, Salonika, Greece." Lewis Wickes Hine, 1918

In the foreground of this photo is a boy who was injured by playing with powder from unexploded amunition.

Refugee families were forced to live in bombed-out buildings until Europe could begin the tremendous job of reconstruction after the end of the war.

In 1919, Hine returned to the United States, where he photographed a
Red Cross nurse visiting a patient in the snows of upper New York State.

ture, Hine portrayed men fixing a road in the town of Hooge, Belgium, which had been destroyed by the war.

As Folks recalled in an article that he wrote for *The World's Work,* "In the fastest auto we traveled for ten days from early morning until dark . . . and saw nothing but devastation. . . . Repeatedly, as we approached a town we thought, 'This place seems to have escaped.' The buildings appeared to be standing, yet as we entered the town and went into the buildings, we found only a ghost of a city." In the town of Lens, France, Hine depicted a lone man surrounded by destruction stretching in every direction. Yet, as the photographer also showed, the French people had already begun to rebuild.

Returning Home

Later in 1919, Hine returned to the United States. His pictures continued to appear in the publications of the American Red Cross. During 1920, Hine was employed by the Red Cross to travel across the United States, taking photographs of the organization's various types of work and arranging these images in exhibits.

But in the aftermath of World War I, America was experiencing an economic downturn. As a result, Hine's work with the Red Cross ended, and he was forced to look for other assignments that took him in new directions.

Hine was fascinated by machines and admired the men who ran them.

CHAPTER SIX

Men at Work

Cities do not build themselves, machines cannot
make machines, unless back of them all are
the brains and toil of men.
—Lewis Hine

"There are two things I wanted to do," Hine once explained. "I wanted to show the things that had to be corrected. I wanted to show the things that had to be appreciated." In his photographs of child laborers, Hine had shown some of the problems in America that needed to be corrected. His pictures of war-torn Europe not only showed conditions that needed to be improved, they shared an appreciation of the spirit demonstrated by Europeans to rebuild their homelands.

Upon his return to the United States following World War I, Hine decided to concentrate on the positive side of American life. The reform movements, where Hine had made his reputation in the past, had declined during the war. After the war ended, in the wake of a conflict that had taken so many lives and caused so much destruction, Americans generally wanted to forget about the negative side of life. They wanted to look forward into a brighter future, and they celebrated it with a frenzy of spending, buying anything and everything, as the economy of the 1920s began to boom.

In this period, known as the Roaring Twenties, industrialization was responsible for the large variety of consumer items that flowed into the marketplace. Machines produced automobiles, refrigerators, record players, and radios. Blast furnaces in large steel mills produced tons of steel to build railroad cars and airplanes and to

erect massive skyscrapers in America's largest cities. Meanwhile, Americans enjoyed themselves, listening to jazz, going to nightclubs, and dancing to fast music.

At first, Hine seemed out of place in the culture of the 1920s. His photographs of children, immigrants, and refugees seemed old fashioned in a society that had lost interest in these subjects. Hine was no longer recognized as one of America's most successful photographers. Indeed, the photographer had trouble finding work, although he did manage to arrange a couple of exhibits of his photographs in New York City to keep his work in front of the public.

However, Hine was not discouraged. Instead, he decided to change direction and try to capture American industrialization on film. But he did not intend to aim his camera at the giant machines or the towering skyscrapers. Hine's subjects, as they had always been, were people—the men who operated the machines, ran the railroads, and constructed the buildings. His goal was "to humanize an inhuman industrial society." He wanted to celebrate the work of his fellow Americans.

In 1921, Hine wrote to Paul Kellogg at the *The Survey*, "I have just finished a series of photographs showing the Human Side of the System . . . the very best thing I have ever done." Among his most powerful photographs were large turbines and transformers being built by men who were shown working right in the middle of them.

As Hine wrote at the time, "Cities do not build themselves, machines cannot make machines, unless back of them all are the brains and toil of men. We call this the Machine Age. But the more machines we use the more do we need real men to make and direct them."

Kellogg praised Hine's work, and some of his pictures appeared in *The Survey*. Among them was a photo of an engineer using a sextant, part of an article titled "Some Tools of the Trade." Another photo portrayed a railroad engineer who had spent forty years in the cab of his locomotive. "The monarch of the rail—throned in his cab. . . . His is the job of self-discipline and self-control, for his mind must be as single-tracked as the rails upon which he is running."

In the early 1920s, however, Kellogg seemed to be one of the few people interested in buying Hine's work. "It will be hard sledding for some time," Hine admitted. "The theme is fundamental and needs to be emphasized in every form of expression." But Hine worried that American industry would not be interested in paying him to produce these pictures.

Opposite: Photographs by Lewis Hine focused on what he called the "human side" of construction work.

Even the largest industrial equipment, Hine realized,
depended on the ingenuity of men to make it work.

Gradually businesses began hiring Hine to take industrial photographs, which
were used in advertising. In 1924, his photograph of the railroad engineer won a
medal for photography given by the prestigious Art Directors Club of New York.
"Two really significant aspects of my work have been recognized by this advertising
award," Hine said, "the acceptance of the appeal of the common man . . . and the

value of the realistic photography." Eight years later, in 1932, Hine published a selection of these photographs in his book, titled *Men At Work*.

In 1928, an exhibition of his work appeared at the Advertising Club in New York, and a year later, Hine was given a special award by the National Child Labor Com-

"Railroad Engineer." Lewis Wickes Hine, 1924

Hine described this photograph as "a mustachioed Pennsylvania railroad engineer [who] leans out the window of his cab, wearing his cap and overalls."

INTERPRETIVE PHOTOGRAPHY

Hine called himself an "interpretive photographer," a term he used in advertisements for his work. This meant that he did not simply photograph what was there. He composed a picture to express his opinion of what he saw and to send a message to his viewers. As Hine explained, "I try to do with the camera what the writer does with words. . . . Unfortunately many persons don't comprehend good writing. On the other hand, a picture makes its appeal to everyone. . . . Interpretive photography . . . will do that, I know, for it has been done."

"In Gear." Lewis Wickes Hine, c. 1934

"A General Electric engineer sitting in the center of an enormous gear casting to measure its bearing."

mittee. In addition, he continued to take photographs at Ellis Island for various clients, such as the Amalgamated Clothing Workers Union, whose members included many immigrants working in the clothing industry. Nevertheless, Hine failed to receive the number of assignments that he had been given a decade earlier, and his business suffered.

The Empire State Building

As a result of wide praise for his industrial photographs, Hine received a very unusual assignment in 1930. He was asked to photograph the construction of the Empire State Building in New York City. Located in the heart of the city, the 102-story skyscraper became the world's tallest building when it was completed in 1931. Hine was hired for this job by the Empire State Corporation, which planned to use the pictures for advertising. He was clearly relieved to have the offer. "Last spring, I was so discouraged with the lack of appreciation of my work that I put our house on the market," he wrote to Paul Kellogg. "Then came this Empire State job and some others that have kept the pot bubbling over."

But a photo documentary of the construction project proved to be a grueling task. Hine was fifty-six years old, and carrying his camera equipment around the construction of the skyscraper would have taxed the energy of a man half his age. Fortunately, he had his son, Corydon, to help him with the equipment. But the job was still extremely dangerous. Hine was afraid of heights but had to follow the workers up the ladders from floor to floor. Then, attached to a safety line, Hine had to balance on steel girders hundreds of feet in the air to capture the men who were working on the building. He photographed them for six months from 1930 to 1931.

His photos included teams of men hoisting cables and girders, cutting the steel supports to the proper size with blowtorches that threw sparks in every direction, positioning them and then riveting them into place, inspecting the work with precision instruments to make sure that it was done correctly. Then, there was the massive task of laying stone and bricks to create the walls of the world's tallest building.

After observing their dangerous work high above the city, Hine later wrote, "Some of them are heroes; all of them persons it is a privilege to know." This was, indeed, the high point of Hine's photographic efforts to portray the strength and nobility of average people doing very important jobs in their everyday work.

HINE ON THE EMPIRE STATE BUILDING

In a letter to Paul Kellogg, Hine described the experience of photographing construction of the world's tallest building:

My six months of skyscraping have culminated in a few extra thrills and finally achieving a record of the Highest Up when I was pushed and pulled up onto the Peak of the Empire State, the highest point yet reached on a man-made structure.

The day before, just before the high derrick was taken down, they swung me out in a box from the hundredth floor (a sheer drop of nearly a quarter of a mile) to get some shots of the tower. The Boss argued that it had never been done and could never be done again. . . .

I have always avoided dare-devil exploits and do not consider these experiences, with the cooperation the men have given me, as going quite that far, but they have given a new zest of high adventure and, perhaps, a different note in my interpretation of Industry.

"Icarus, high up on Empire State." Lewis Wickes Hine, c. 1938

Hine climbed to the top of the Empire State Building
to take some of his most remarkable photos.

Constructing the Empire State
Building in New York City.

"Drought victim, boy from Kentucky," Lewis Wickes Hine, c. 1930

The Great Depression devastated the lives of many American families, leaving them in terrible poverty.

CHAPTER SEVEN

The Great Depression

These photographs were taken primarily as records.
They are direct and simple. The presence in them of
an emotional quality raises them to works of art.
—Beaumont Newhall

While Lewis Hine was working on his photographs of the Empire State Building, America plunged into a severe economic downturn known as the Great Depression. The Depression began in October 1929, when the New York Stock Exchange experienced an enormous drop. Many people had invested in stocks during the 1920s. With the crash of the stock market, businesses began to go bankrupt, banks closed, and many people lost all of their savings.

As the U.S. economy declined, approximately 25 percent of all workers lost their jobs. Men who had formerly earned enough to support their families were forced to sell pencils or apples on the street to make what little money they could. Others waited at churches that provided free meals for the long lines of unemployed. Meanwhile, a severe drought struck the Midwest, as the results of years of overfarming and unusually dry weather turned fertile farmland into a vast Dust Bowl, forcing many farmers to abandon their land.

With the onset of the Depression, Hine's own photographic assignments began to decline, and *The Survey* purchased fewer of his pictures. In 1931, however, he was hired by the American Red Cross to photograph the terrible drought that was affecting farmers in Arkansas and Kentucky. His son Corydon became Hine's assistant and continued to work with him during the 1930s.

In 1931, the Yonkers Art Museum held an exhibit of Hine's work—the best ever presented—and the photographer was very excited. As he wrote to Arthur Kellogg, "[I've] been having the biggest showing I ever had of my 'quarter-century of work,' at the

A woman in Tennessee looks at a field devastated by flooding. In 1933, President Franklin Delano Roosevelt created the Tennessee Valley Authority (TVA) in order to build dams on the Tennessee River as flood control and to bring electricity to rural people.

Yonkers Art Museum, recently, with a lot of good newspaper appreciation. *American Magazine* is planning to run a story with a bunch of old favorites [Hine's pictures] soon."

After Hine's book *Men at Work* was published in 1932, the photographer received a commission from Sidney Bloomenthal, the owner of the Shelton Looms manufacturing company. The next year, Hine photographed the mill workers at their looms, and several of his pictures appeared in *The Survey*. In 1933, he published a portfolio of his pictures, *Through the Threads of the Shelton Looms,* and sent copies of the photographs to the Museum of Modern Art and the Metropolitan Museum of Art in New York City.

Photography for the Federal Government

As the Great Depression grew worse, Americans demanded that Congress and Republican president Herbert Hoover provide new legislation that would put people back to work. But Hoover did very little, believing that the economic downturn would end by itself, as other depressions had in the past.

The Roosevelt administration started projects such as the Tennessee Valley Authority to help farmers recover.

The Red Cross, schools, and other organizations fed some of the families suffering during the Depression.

Opposite: "Flooding carried away the fish spawn in the beds of the Tennessee river." "TVA projects in the Kentucky Lake dam." Ralph Crane, 1952

"Typical colored school near Shaw, Mississippi." Lewis Wickes Hine, 1930 or 1931

As a result of Hoover's inaction, voters elected Democrat Franklin D. Roosevelt as president in 1932. Roosevelt promised a New Deal, offering programs that would provide employment for millions of out-of-work Americans. The Roosevelt administration eventually organized a variety of programs, such as the Civilian Conservation Corps (CCC) and the Works Progress Administration (WPA). The CCC put young men to work preserving America's national forests and other natural resources, while the WPA gave unemployed workers jobs building roads and bridges.

Part of Roosevelt's New Deal was the Tennessee Valley Authority (TVA). Begun in 1933, the TVA helped farmers who lived in the Tennessee River Valley to use fertilizers and other methods to improve their crops. Among the biggest projects of the TVA was the construction of dams that would create hydro-electric power to provide electricity to thousands of farmers in the Tennessee River Valley.

Because of the success of his portfolio for Shelton Looms, Hine was hired in 1933 by the TVA to photograph one of the dam construction projects in the Tennessee River Valley. He spent a month photographing the Wilson and Muscle Shoals Dam for $1,000 plus his expenses. "Have had a glorious month with the TVA," Hine wrote. But after this brief assignment he left because of a disagreement with Dr. Arthur Morgan, the man who had hired him. Morgan wanted to use the photographs primarily to illustrate the charts and drawings of the dam. Hine, on the other hand, wanted the photographs to be used as publicity for the dam projects. Morgan also used Hine's photographs without mentioning his name in the TVA's printed material, which irritated the photographer.

Hine also had hoped to work for the Farm Security Administration (FSA), another agency established under the New Deal. He repeatedly contacted Roy Stryker, who ran the FSA. But after his experience with the TVA, Hine had gained a reputation as someone who was a "true artist type" and "requires handling as such," which meant that he was difficult to deal with.

As a result, Hine was never hired by Stryker. Hine regretted being turned down by the FSA. Stryker hired some of America's finest photographers, such as Dorothea Lange and Walker Evans. Their pictures of poor farmers, designed to publicize the impact of the Dust Bowl, were among the most moving photographs taken during the Great Depression. Photographers such as Lange and Evans were continuing a style of photography that had been pioneered by Lewis Hine. But while they were widely praised for their work, Hine was largely overlooked.

Nevertheless, Hine was successful in landing a short assignment with the Rural Electrification Administration. In 1935, he traveled through Pennsylvania, Ohio, and New

DOROTHEA LANGE AND WALKER EVANS

Two of the most successful photographers during the Great Depression were Dorothea Lange and Walker Evans. Born in 1895, Lange studied photography in New York City before moving to San Francisco, where she worked as a portrait photographer. During the 1930s, she was hired by New Deal agencies to photograph families who had lost their farms. She provided these pictures to newspapers to publicize the hardships of average Americans. In a famous photograph of a farm worker and her children, Lange said, "I saw and approached the hungry and desperate mother, as if drawn by a magnet. . . . She said that they had been living on frozen vegetables from the surrounding fields, and birds that the children had killed."

Walker Evans also was employed by New Deal agencies, and many of his most famous pictures portray poor farm families. Born in Missouri in 1903, he later moved to New York and, during the 1930s, began doing photographic work in West Virginia and Pennsylvania. In the early 1940s, he published a book with author James Agee called *Let Us Now Praise Famous Men*, featuring his photographs of America's farmers.

"Floyd Burroughs, sharecropper." Walker Evans, 1935 or 1936

"Destitute pea pickers in California, Nipomo, California." Dorothea Lange, 1936

Walker Evans photographed farmers, such as this sharecropper, who lost their land in the Depression.

Dorothea Lange's photos expressed the desperation and courage of families who had lost everything.

York, shooting photographs along the way. The following year, Hine was hired for a short period as chief photographer for the National Research Project of the WPA. Approximately 2.5 million people were employed each month by the WPA.

As Hine wrote to Paul Kellogg, "Thus far it has been just one adventure after another, and the beginning of what seems to be the most glorious visual joyride I've had since the old days of Child Laboring and Red Crossing." Nevertheless, the work for the WPA paid far less than Hine had been used to earning in the past. In addition, he had not been successful in selling any photographs to journals or magazines. As a result, Hine and his wife were struggling financially.

Last Years

Finally, good luck came his way. In 1938, Hine showed his photographs to Beaumont Newhall, the curator of the Museum of Modern Art, who had recently run an exhibit about the history of photography. Newhall was so impressed with Hine's work that he wrote an article about him for the *Magazine of Art*. "These photographs were taken primarily as records," Newhall wrote. "They are direct and simple. The presence in them of an emotional quality raises them to works of art. 'Photo Interpretations,' Hine calls them. He might well have called them 'documentary photographs.'"

As a result of the article, Hine was hired to work on a project for CBS radio about American workers. "The broadcast may be called *Men at Work*," Hine wrote to Paul Kellogg. Nevertheless, this project provided only a small amount of money, and Hine continued to search for additional work.

Meanwhile, the Newhall article led to renewed interest in Hine's photography. Late in 1938, the Riverside Museum in New York organized an exhibit of Hine's work. At the same time, articles about Hine appeared in *The Survey* and *U.S. Camera Annual*. In a letter to art critic Elizabeth McCausland, who wrote the articles, Hine said, "Every new product from you gives me a catch in my breath and a lump in my throat and an increased wonderment."

After the exhibit opened in January 1939, good reviews helped Hine obtain work. Hine's photo story on a railroad engineer appeared in the June issue of *Fortune* magazine—a prestigious business publication. One of Hine's photos appeared in an issue of *Life*, a national weekly magazine that featured photo stories.

But this work was hardly enough for Hine and his family to pay their bills. Late in 1939, Hine's wife, Sara, died of pneumonia. The Hines had always enjoyed a very close relationship, and Sara had assisted Lewis in his work. After her loss, he never really recovered. Lewis Hine became ill in 1940 and died on November 4 in New York.

A group portrait of boys smiling and sitting in front
of a building with their arms around each other.

Legacy of Lewis Hine

When Lewis Hine died in 1940, his work had largely been forgotten. Nevertheless, he
had laid the foundation for a style of photography that became widely used during his
own lifetime and would become even more popular after his death. Hine was a documentary photographer—telling a story through his photographs. His approach was so
new that he had to invent his own terms to describe it—terms such as photo story and
time exposure. Hine recognized the powerful combination created by words and photographs. And photo stories became widely used in weekly magazines, like *Life*, and in
news magazines, such as *Time* and *Newsweek*.

But Hine was more than a photographer—he was also a teacher, trying to raise the
consciousness level of his audiences, enabling them to see the injustice that existed in
their own country, and urging them to act and correct it. An unusual combination of
teacher, artist, and photographer, Hine produced some of America's most unforget-
table photographs, creating timeless images that remain as powerful today as they were
a century ago.

GLOSSARY

Dust Bowl—A description of conditions caused by overfarming and severe drought that led to many families in the Midwest having to leave their farms during the 1930s.

Ellis Island—The point of entry in New York Harbor for most immigrants who came by ship from Europe to the United States between 1892 and 1954.

Ethical Culture School—A high school in New York City that offered academic courses and vocational training to the children of immigrants.

Great Depression—The severe collapse of the U.S. economy that affected all Americans, beginning in 1929.

Hull House—A community center or settlement house in Chicago that offered educational programs and other support to newly arrived immigrants.

Interpretive photography—Photographs taken with the intent of expressing an opinion about their subjects.

Magic lantern—An early type of slide projector.

Muckraker—A journalist who exposes dishonesty in business and government through his or her published works.

National Child Labor Committee (NCLC)—An organization founded in 1905 with the goal of eliminating child labor in the United States.

New Deal—The programs and promises that Franklin D. Roosevelt started between 1933 and 1938 to provide relief to the poor, help reform of the financial system, and boost the recovery of the economy during the Great Depression.

Photojournalist—A reporter who tells a story through photographs.

Photo story—A visual documentary with words and photographs.

Red Cross—An international humanitarian movement with millions of volunteers worldwide whose mission is to protect human life and health, to ensure respect for human beings, and to prevent and alleviate human suffering.

Settlement house—A facility established in a major city to provide education and other programs for the poor.

State Normal School—A teachers' college located in Oshkosh, Wisconsin.

Time exposure—An arrangement of pictures in various shapes and sizes that are presented with an accompanying article that puts them in time context.

Vocational training—Courses that teach people skills they need to perform various jobs.

Works Progress Administration (WPA)—The largest New Deal agency, created in 1935 by Franklin D. Roosevelt. The WPA employed millions of people, who built public buildings, bridges, and roads and operated large arts, drama, media, and literacy projects during the Great Depression.

TIME LINE

1874: Lewis Hine is born on September 16 in Oshkosh, Wisconsin.

1892: Hine's father is accidentally killed; Lewis goes to work.

1893: An economic depression grips the United States.

1901: Hine goes to New York City to teach at the Ethical Culture School.

1904: Hine marries Sara Rich in Oshkosh. He begins photographing immigrants on Ellis Island in New York Harbor.

1906: Hine starts working for the National Child Labor Committee (NCLC).

1908: Hine leaves the Ethical Culture School to become a professional photographer.

1910: The NCLC hires Hine as a full-time photographer.

1911–1917: Hine continues taking pictures for the NCLC.

1914–1918: World War I rages across Europe.

1918–1919: The American Red Cross hires Hine, and he photographs war-torn Europe.

1924: The Art Directors Club awards Hine a medal for his photograph of an engineer.

1929: Hine receives a special award from the NCLC. The Great Depression begins.

1930–1931: Hine photographs the construction of the Empire State Building.

1931: An exhibit of Hine's photographs is held at Yonkers Art Museum. The American Red Cross hires Hine to photograph effects of the Dust Bowl on American farmers.

1932: Hine publishes *Men at Work*. Franklin D. Roosevelt is elected as president.

1933: President Roosevelt's plan the New Deal begins. Hine works for the Tennessee Valley Authority (TVA)

1935: The Rural Electrification Administration hires Hine.

1936: The Works Progress Administration (WPA) hires Hine.

1938: The Riverside Museum in New York organizes an exhibit of Hine's work.

1939: Hine's wife, Sara, dies of pneumonia.

1940: Lewis Hine dies in New York on November 4.

FURTHER RESEARCH

BOOKS AND VIDEOS

America and Lewis Hine. Video. New York: Daedalus Productions, 1996.

Campbell Bartoletti, Susan. *Growing Up in Coal Country.* New York: Houghton Mifflin, 1996.

Freedman, Russell. *Kids at Work: Lewis Hine and the Crusade Against Child Labor.* New York: Clarion, 1994.

Hine, Lewis W. *Men At Work: 69 Classic Photographs by Lewis W. Hine.* Mineola, NY: Dover, 1977.

ARTICLES

Gilgoff, Dan. "Shedding Light on Dark Corners." *U.S. News & World Report,* July 9, 2001.

Goldberg, Vicki. "No Choice But Work." *Civilization,* January/February 1996.

"Scandal Exposed! A Photographer Goes Undercover to Shed Light on the Evils of Child Labor." *Scholastic Update,* November 3, 1995.

Winthrop, Elizabeth. "Through the Mill." *Smithsonian,* September 2006.

WEB SITES

Addie Card: The Search for an Anemic Little Spinner
www.morningsonmaplestreet.com/addiesearch2.html.

Hull House
www.spartacus.schoolnet.co.uk/USAhullhouse.htm.

BIBLIOGRAPHY

Goldberg, Vicki. *Lewis W. Hine: Children at Work*. Munich: Prestel-Verlag, 1999.

Hine, Lewis W. *Empire State Building*. Ed. Freddy Langer. Munich, Germany: Prestel-Verlang, 1988.

———. *Men at Work: 69 Classic Photographs by Lewis Hine*. Mineola, NY: Dover, 1977.

Kaplan, Daile. *Lewis Hine in Europe: The Lost Photographs*. New York: Abbeville, 1988.

———, ed. *Photo Story: Selected Letters and Photographs of Lewis W. Hine*. Washington, DC: Smithsonian Institution, 1993.

Rosenblum, Walter, et al. *America and Lewis Hine*. New York: Aperture, 1977.

SOURCE NOTE

Many of the direct quotations from Hine's writing that appear in this book—especially those from his letters—can be found in Daile Kaplan's *Photo Story: Selected Letters and Photographs of Lewis W. Hine*. You can see sixty of Hine's photographs with his original captions at the History Place site: www.historyplace.com/unitedstates/childlabor/.

INDEX

ABOUT THE AUTHOR

Richard Worth, a Connecticut-based writer, is the author of more than fifty books for young adults. They include biographies, histories and books on current events and on family living. He is a collector of American Impressionist paintings by Connecticut artists from the Old Lyme School.

PHOTO CREDITS

The photographs in this book are used by permission and through the courtesy of: